Wishing
you a lifetime
of love and
simple pleasures!

Ordering Information:
www.Etsy.com/ClarionKidBooks
www.Amazon.com

For details, contact pam.rak@ctechrocks.com

Print ISBN: 978-1-7365309-2-4
eBook ISBN: 978-1-7365309-3-1

Printed in the United States of America on SFI Certified paper.

First Edition

The simplest pleasures
are our greatest treasures.

— Pam Selker Rak

Cover illustration based on original photo from George Wolf, Jr.

Christmas TREEDITION

written by PAM SELKER RAK

illustrated by Susan Vincent
designed by Lindsay Johnson

Every year, around the same date,
My dad would say, "Come on now, let's not be late!"
To the truck I'd run with sheer delight,
We had to go while it was still daylight.

With an axe and a saw tucked under his arm,
We were off to the local Christmas tree farm.
All the way down, we'd strategize,
Which row to tackle first, we'd analyze.

"I want the tallest one!" I'd tell my dad,
"And the roundest one, too!" I liked to add.
Dad listened patiently as he drove the car,
Then reminded me we had to leave room for the star.

At last, we arrived and turned down the lane.
We did it by memory, the road had no name.
There were pine trees everywhere, to the left and the right,
And the little white farmhouse was in plain sight.

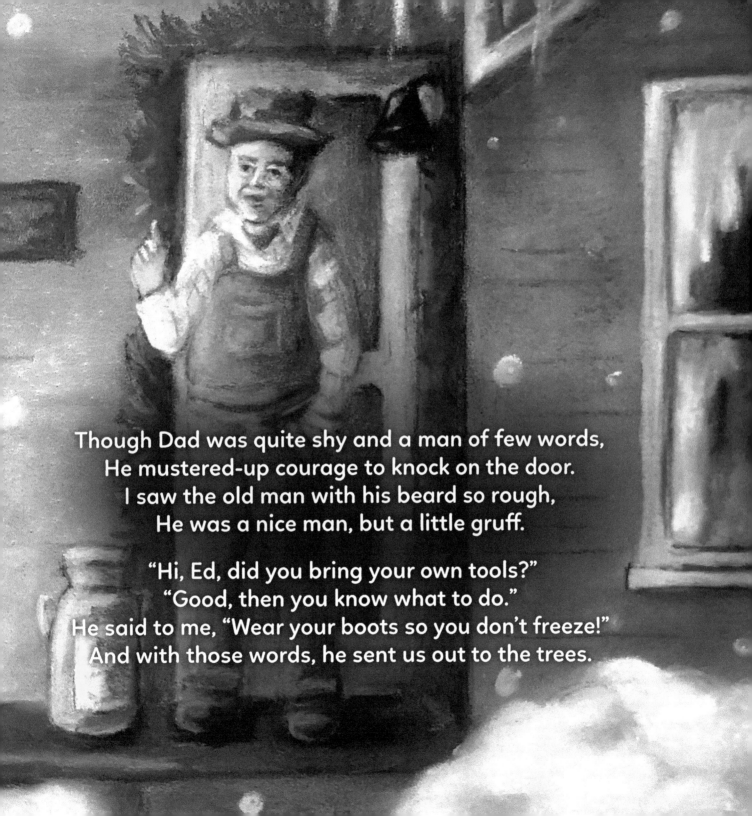

Though Dad was quite shy and a man of few words,
He mustered-up courage to knock on the door.
I saw the old man with his beard so rough,
He was a nice man, but a little gruff.

"Hi, Ed, did you bring your own tools?"
"Good, then you know what to do."
He said to me, "Wear your boots so you don't freeze!"
And with those words, he sent us out to the trees.

We explored every inch of that magical field,
Knowing our tree would soon be revealed.
The field looked flush with green wallpaper,
And the pines towered over me like city skyscrapers!

"How about this one?" dad asked me.
"This looks like a really good tree."
"It's lean and straight and has a good trunk,"
"It will fit in our window and into our truck."

I looked it over but wasn't convinced.
"It's not round enough," I had to persist.
"Let's keep looking," I begged my dad.
He was so patient and never got mad!

So off we'd go to another row,
And there it was, covered in snow!
The fattest tree I'd ever seen,
Topped off with the deepest color of green.

Dad gave me a look, he was dubious,
But he saw how I loved it, that was obvious.
The branches were sparse and the trunk, quite crooked.
It wasn't ideal, but he was tired of looking.

So the sawing and chopping soon began,
And the tree fell to the ground with a whoosh, whirl and a bang.
We dragged it out and wrestled it to the truck
And my dad paid the old man fifteen bucks.

When we got the tree home, my mom had to check it.
From top-to-bottom, she'd inspect it.
"I don't think it's going to fit!"
"But it will be fine once we decorate it."

Once dad got it secured, we kids took over,
With bulbs and tinsel, and nothing leftover.
And when it was finished, like a Christmas tableau,
It glimmered and shimmered in our picture window!

With each passing year, when I decorate my tree,
My mind wanders back to those days fondly.
No matter how old, I find myself wishing,
That I could have one more year of our

Christmas "Treedition!"

Proceeds from this Book
Will Be Donated to:

Jefferson Clarion

EST. HEAD START, INC. 1981

JEFFERSON-CLARION HEAD START, INC.

Jefferson-Clarion Head Start, Inc. is a private non-profit corporation that serves as the administrative entity for child and family development programs including Head Start, Early Head Start, Maternal, Infant, Early Childhood Home Visiting (MIECHV), the PA Pilot Home Visiting Program-Opiate Use Disorder/Substance Use Disorder, and Parents as Teachers (PAT). Each of these programs has our fundamental mission at its core which is to provide comprehensive services to children and families. Jefferson-Clarion Head Start, Inc. has been providing quality comprehensive services to nearly 700 children each year in both Jefferson and Clarion Counties in Western Pennsylvania for thirty-nine (39) years.

Our Mission Statement: Jefferson-Clarion Head Start, Inc. is dedicated to providing comprehensive education and health services to income eligible children to ensure they will be healthier and better prepared for success in school and life. We seek to promote family self-sufficiency by providing educational opportunities to parents and establishing family partnerships designed to build upon the strengths of each family. We are committed to collaborating effectively with schools, child care providers, and other social service agencies while being responsive to the changing needs of our communities.

MEET THE CREATORS

PAM SELKER RAK, author
The Reasons Behind Her Rhymes

Back in 1969, a little girl who was growing-up in a little town, descended a flight of stairs and entered a world that would change her life forever: The Clarion Free Public Library, nestled snugly in the little Main Street of Clarion, Pennsylvania.

From a little seat at a little table, she surrounded herself with books, and something magical started to occur: her imagination grew and grew and grew some more.

Throughout her life, words and poems became her constant companion. When she was bored, she read. When she started school, she started writing. When she went to college, she studied communications. When she graduated, words became her career, her hobby, and her solace. And now, words have become her memories, and her mission.

All proceeds from her children's books are donated to nonprofit organizations serving Pennsylvania's communities, and especially children. From her entrepreneurial training and civic leadership passion, Rak firmly believes that our communities need us now more than ever. By purchasing one of Rak's books, you, too, are supporting important community organizations like public libraries and early education programs.

Christmas Treedition is the second in a series of children's books that offer a fast-paced world a few minutes to slow down. Long before video games, social media and mobile devices were simple pleasures. In Rak's first book, *Sassafras Tea*, a little girl learns from her father how to turn a tree into tea! There is nothing simpler, or more magical, than that.

In *Christmas Treedition*, that same little girl goes on an annual trek with her father to a towering forest of pine trees, in search of the perfect one to fill their family's picture window for the holiday season. As you read this book with the children in your life, you'll literally imagine the smell of the pines, you'll feel the cool, crisp air as it reddens your cheeks, you'll hear the crunch of the snow under your boots, and you'll feel tiny little snowflakes fall gently on the tip of your nose!

Rak hopes her books rekindle the fond family memories we all have, especially during the holidays. And above all, she hopes her books remind us that the simplest pleasures are truly our greatest treasures.

SUSAN E. VINCENT, illustrator

Susan Vincent is an illustrator from Pittsburgh with over thirty years of freelance and artistic experience. Her work has included everything from t-shirt and business card designs to wall-sized murals, and everything in between. She enjoys mostly doing portraits, working in pastel and oil, and has been drawing and creating for as long as she can remember. She comes from a family of artistic people and credits her mom for being her inspiration with her own creative endeavors throughout the years.

Her mission in her business and life is to convey a sense of joi de vivre - the exultation of spirit and enjoyment of life - and enjoys being a part of helping others discover and develop their creativity. She has taught painting, drawing and portrait classes, but her most rewarding experiences were early in her career working with first-time authors and staff at a small publishing company in Baden, PA, designing inspirational book covers.

Susan is a graduate of the Art Institute of Pittsburgh and took art classes at Carnegie Mellon University, while still in grade school. She has her own business, Emerald Elf Design, and loves working in her she-shed studio.

LINDSAY T. JOHNSON, graphic designer

Lindsay Johnson is a Pittsburgh based freelance graphic designer. She has enjoyed a full career of more than twenty-five years.

She enjoys working with a variety of clients on an even larger array of projects. She loves seeing the stages of a project develop from an initial thought to a final deliverable. It is exciting to help someone communicate their message in a creative effect way – and most importantly make it look great too!

She is most thankful that her successful freelance career has allowed her to raise her three children Derian, Kadsen and Korvyn while working from her home-based office...WAY before home-based offices were the "new normal".

Lindsay is a graduate of LaRoche University. She has her own business, Lindsay Johnson Designhaus.

No matter how you celebrate, treasure the love of the holiday season!

HAPPY KWANZAA!

HAPPY HANUKKAH!

MERRY CHRISTMAS!

HAPPY HOLIDAYS!

CPSIA information can be obtained
at www.ICGtesting.com
Printed in the USA
BVHW020226050921
616061BV00001B/1